Overcoming the Odds

Overcoming the Odds

The Story of Courage, Resilience and Triumph

CELESTE

Rev. date: 02/22/2019

To order additional copies of this book, contact:
Xlibris
1-888-795-4274
www.Xlibris.com
Orders@Xlibris.com
792213

Dedication

This book is dedicated in loving memory to my late grandmother who passed away on June 19, 2017, and my late grandfather who passed away in 1991. It is because of their nurturing love, guidance and prayers for me throughout the years in my life, that I am where I am today.

Disclosure

This book is based upon true events which have taken place within the life of a young woman named Celeste.

Some or all of the names in this book have been changed, to respect the individual/s right to privacy.

Personal Statement

I am a first time published author, who felt compelled to write this book, for several reasons. The first being, the Creator gave me the "gift" of writing and I finally began to embrace that gift.

The Creator put the desire both in my mind and heart to write all that I have experienced throughout my life, because with it I can bring "healing and encouragement" to the countless other women and men who has suffered with similar stories.

The beauty of the testimony I have is that, you would never know my story, until now when I decide to share with you. The resilience and strength that I had to overcome and not become another statistic.

I kept hearing for so many years throughout my educational, professional and personal life what a good writer I was, and lastly, I thought to myself, if I can help to bring hope, healing and empowerment to even just one individual or multiple individuals, both women and men who may have experienced some "unresolved trauma" throughout their life, it's well worth it, one of the many reasons I decided to pursue entering the field of social work.

Unfortunately, we are not able to decide the cards we are dealt in life, as far as parents, family, etc.., and regardless to whatever pain we may have suffered as a child or throughout our life in general, we can ultimately regain control of our lives and turn something in which we thought was so tragic throughout our lives for a positive, which can bring encouragement, strength and resilience in the lives of those we encounter throughout our lives.

My prayer is that you as the reader go throughout the chapters in this book and throughout the story of my life, that it provide you with a sense of hope and peace that no matter where you are presently in life, or what you may have went through in your life, that it does not define your future. You have the ability to regain control, regain your life and ultimately change your future. Your past as painful as it may have been, is exactly that, "YOUR PAST". It does "NOT" define your future. And always remember, that "YOU" can turn that pain, into something for good. Healing and hope to yourself and others.

I hope you enjoy the book!

Chapter One

Celeste was born on April, 1972 in New York City, NY to teenage parents named Marvin and Kay. Marvin was seventeen years old at the time and Kay was fifteen. Marvin and Kay both were born and raised in Amsterdam Houses, which is located in NYC.

Both Marvin and Kay were inexperienced and lacked the knowledge on parenting, as they were both children themselves. Kay lived in an overcrowded two- bedroom tenement building with her father Benjamin, her mother Ann, her sister Terry, her niece Tonya and her daughter Celeste.

Marvin was in his senior year of high school, and was as the top his game in his basketball, with promising wishes for success, after receiving a full scholarship for basketball. Kay was a sophomore getting ready to enter into her junior year when Celeste was born.

With both Marvin and Kay having their own lives, they had no time for raising Celeste. Marvin was on his way off to college with a full scholarship for basketball and was adamant at pursuing his dreams up hopefully getting picked up by the NBA, and Kay simply just wanted to hang out and party with her friends. Celeste always felt a sense of resentment and bitterness coming from Kay, her mother, as a result of her being born.

The resentment that Celeste felt coming from Kay, was as a result of the lack of time she spent with her and always choosing to prefer the company of men, as opposed to spending time with Celeste. In addition, it was told to Celeste later on when she was an adult, that Kay would lie

to her boyfriends' and tell them that Celeste was her sibling as opposed to being her child.

There continued to be speculation throughout the years amongst family and friends of the possibility of another female sibling who was given up for adoption; however Celeste's searches always came up empty. In addition, Kay never acknowledged this "other child" and in fact, adamantly denied on several occasions, of not having this "other child", so only the Creator knows the real story behind that.

Celeste's grandparents Benjamin and Ann played a significant role in the overall raising and the upbringing for her and other siblings, throughout their childhood years. While Kay was always out running the streets and partying with her friends and men. Celeste's grandparents took the responsibility of ensuring that Celeste and her siblings had everything they needed, in order to be taken care of.

Celeste's Grandfather Benjamin was the sole bread winner, and took the responsibility of paying all of the bills, where Celeste's Grandmother Ann, was a housewife, who took responsibility of caring for the household duties, that included taking care of the house and children.

Celeste was very close to both of her grandparents and had a close bond with them both. She was so close with her grandfather Benjamin, that she called him "Dad", instead of grandpa, and she called her Grandmother, "Mama". It was where she felt safe, and who she knew in her heart or hearts that loved her, and couldn't have imagined life without them.

Celeste's grandmother Ann was known in every school that Celeste and her siblings attended, as "Grandma". This was because Ann always walked Celeste and her siblings to school every day, volunteered throughout the school day at the school and waited until it was time to for them to be dismissed, for them all to walk home together.

Celeste and her siblings weren't always so happy about being dropped off and picked up to school by their grandmother, especially when they got older. You know how it is, once you start approaching the pre-teen and adolescent years, it's no longer "cool" to hang out with

parents, you just want to hang out with your friends. However, present day, with Celeste now being an adult, now recognizes that, at that time in her life, it was one of her biggest blessings and pleasant memorable moments throughout her difficult life.

Chapter Two

Celeste always use to love school and was always at the top of her class with her grades and studies. It was during Celeste's early years in her life, that she had aspirations and dreams of becoming a "school teacher". She would always play school with her younger siblings, along with some teddy bears and dolls to be her students. Celeste always enjoyed playing school, and would play for her hours, especially since she was always the teacher. Those were one of the pleasant memories in Celeste's life.

One of Celeste's other pleasant memories from her childhood, included summer visits to stay at her god-father and cousin's house during the summer months, when school was out of session. Being at her extended family's house, offered to help bring her a sense of peace and stability, something her young parents could not provide for her at the time.

There were many times that Celeste would feel bad, and sometimes saddened of her cousin. Reason being, is her cousin had two parents who loved her and would do anything for her. Celeste would sometimes find herself questioning God, as to why she too couldn't have two parents who love her the same. Celeste was very family oriented and wanted desperately for her family to be together, however, it always appeared to be an issue.

Celeste had just turned twelve years old, and it was at this time, that Kay had re-connected back with her sibling's father Brian Sr.. They were planning to get married and expecting their fifth child. When Kay decided, it was time for change, and onto a "better" life. Both Kay

and Raphael were looking for better for themselves and their children. Brian Sr. was good for Kay, he was family oriented and helped to slow Kay down from her partying ways, and this however, would be very short lived.

So, Kay and Brian Sr. moved to New Jersey. Celeste initially wasn't happy about this, after all, New York was all she has known, and all of her friends from school were in New York, however over time, Celeste was able to adjust and develop another routine that worked for out in New Jersey, In addition, she made some new friends.

When Celeste turned twelve, tragedy struck. Celeste experienced having to endure one of the hardest losses of her life that she could have experienced at that time. Her grandfather Benjamin passed away. Benjamin had been suffering with multiple issues with his health; this was due to is issues he suffered with his drinking. It was speculated that because of the disappointment he was suffering with, as a result of Kay not achieving his hopes and dreams for her to be fulfilled, the tension, and tumultuous relationship between his two daughters Kay and h Terry, helped to push him along to increase his alcohol intake, which unfortunately, took his life away far too soon.

One of Celeste's greatest fears had taken place, she had lost her grandfather. What was Celeste going to do now? She felt so lost, and suffered during the bereavement process. In Celeste's eyes, she felt like she had lost more than a grand-father, but more like she lost her "Dad", as she always called him. Who was going to protect her now? She felt as though she just wanted to give up, and asked the Creator to take her home, just so she can see her grand-father again.

Celeste struggled throughout this time and it was difficult for her, she couldn't understand why her grand-father had to go. That next year, Celeste graduated from the eighth grade. However she had a relationship with the Creator and the love of her grandmother, which ultimately helped her to overcome and get through it.

Chapter Three

After the passing of Benjamin, things were different for a while and actually went quite well. Kay had actually stepped a little bit. She had gotten a good government job and was working things out with her second and third child's father Brian Sr.

Brian Sr. was two years older than Kay, however he was always hardworking, mature and a family man, who accepted Celeste as his own. Brian Sr. helped to keep Kay balanced for a while. Kay still had her moment where she wanted to go partying with her friends, and still live the life of a teenager.

The differences of opinions, the likes and dislikes of one another's views, helped to contribute too many disagreements and arguments amongst the young couple. Brian Sr. tried so desperately to try and keep his family together. His family meant the world to hi, and he would stop at nothing to keep it.

This helped to bring some sense of greater stability to Celeste. For the first time in her life, since her grandfather passed, she felt like she had another father figure around. Brian Sr. was employed at a local Toys R Us store as an Assistant Manager, and was making good money, while Kay had started working with the federal government and was also making good money.

Things couldn't have appeared to be better. Things appeared to be slowly falling into place and off to a good start. Kay was starting to become more independent, and taking responsibility for herself and the kids.

Brian Sr. was no longer a fan of the "city" life anymore, and was seeking more of the suburb life. That's when he and Kay had decided to uproot the family to New Jersey, with the hopes for a better life and a new beginning. A new beginning it was for a while, until it was the beginning of the end.

Celeste along with her siblings was initially not happy with the move to New Jersey, because they had all their friends in New York. However, over time, they began to make new friends and as long Celeste had her "Mama" around, she would be good wherever she was. During this time, Celeste felt a sense of stability for herself and her siblings.

It is during this time, that Celeste, along with her siblings and her stepfather Brian Sr., who always appeared to be the more mature parent, the "family man", would take Kay, Celeste, her younger siblings Brian Sr., Mignon and Janelle and her "Mama" on weekend trips, vacations, etc.. It was always about family time for Brian Sr., and Celeste and her siblings loved this about him.

Kay went on to marry Brian Sr. in a ceremony witnessed by family and friends, and for once it felt like a "real family' for Celeste and her siblings. Kay went on to have her last female child Arianna. This sense of stability and comfort would soon come to an end. This sense of "peace" which was once foreign coming from Kay would come to a screeching halt.

Kay was able to stay somewhat responsible and help to maintain the family from a financial standpoint through her employment. However, the "party girl" life for Kay wasn't too far behind, and life as she knew it with Brian Sr. began to get to predictable and boring for her. She wanted to live her life and live it freely.

It was always obvious to others, that Kay had a sense of bitterness and resentment towards Celeste and her first four children that she had while she was a teenager. She always use to say, her childhood was cut short, as a result of having children so young, and many ways her selfishness and actions always seem to portray her inner feelings of bitterness and resentment towards Celeste and her younger siblings.

Chapter Four

As time begins to passes, life appears to be as routine, until Celeste's grandmother, "Mama" gets a phone call, with some disturbing news from her aunt Bara. Apparently, Bara is having some financial difficulties as a single parent trying to raise her three children. So as result, Celeste's grandmother Ann decides to go to Georgia at the time, where her Aunt Bara was living, in an effort to try and help her get back on her feet.

Celeste was devastated by this news, and wanted to go so badly with her grandmother, but her "Mama" pleaded with her to finish up with school, as she was doing so well. She explained to Celeste that she did not want to uproot and disturb her studies, but ensured her that it would be for short time and then she would return. Celeste and her grandmother spoke every day, however life as Celeste knew it, would never be the same.

Immediately after Celeste's grandmother left to go down to Georgia to help her aunt Bara, Kay's old party girl ways returned. She begins to start staying out later and later and eventually progressed to her not coming home at all. This ultimately left Celeste to be in charge of herself and her younger siblings while her stepfather Brian Sr. was at work.

As time went on, things only begin to spiral more and more out of control. There were speculations of infidelity on both sides for Kay and Brian Sr., however Brian Sr., still continued to at least support the household and did come every night, however Kay didn't. This caused many arguments between Brian and Sr., which ultimately led to the

cops being called and Brian Sr. being forced to exit out of his own home by the police.

After Brian Sr. was forced out of his own home by the police, he desperately tried to keep in contact with Celeste and her younger siblings; however his efforts were always met with failure. He tried through the court system; however the court was not on his side. Because he was so abruptly put out, and didn't have his own apartment, he was found to be "unfit" to be able to gain custody of the children, so Celeste and her younger siblings were forced to have to stay with their mother Kay.

Once it was evident that Brian Sr. was out of the house and would be unable to return, due to police escort, Kay brought home her new boyfriend Arnold, the one she had been sneaking around with while she had been married to Brian Sr., Kay moved Arnold into the home immediately around her three teenage daughters, teenage son and three year old daughter at the time, despite family members and friends concern and caution against this.

The reason that both many friends and family members were against this, is for several reasons. The first being, that there was no time for healing and adjustment for Celeste and her siblings, after the separation of their parents. The second reason for concern, was the fact that all of her children with exception of one, was females and teenagers. And lastly, the third concern, was due to the fact that they Celeste and her siblings knew absolutely nothing about this man.

Despite family members' arguments and concerns, Kay refused to listen, causing long term friendships and relationships with family members to come to an end. Looking back, Celeste states that she now sees it was ultimately apart of Arnold's plan too separate the family, and bring them into a state of isolation, so he wouldn't have to explain himself to many.

Kay wasted no time with moving Arnold into their home with Celeste and her siblings. Within twenty four hours to be exact. Kay had come to the decision that she was going to make herself the priority, and that her happiness came first. It was a decision that ultimately would later turn to be catastrophic for the family as whole.

Celeste didn't get a good vibe from Arnold; however she didn't have a choice but to accept him, because Kay wouldn't have it any other way. If Celeste and her siblings didn't accept him, they would be either beaten with a belt for being "disobedient" and going against "God's word "or kicked out of the home. The thing that no one knew at the time was that Arnold was a pedophile in disguise, just waiting for the perfect opportunity to strike his plan of action to forever change the lives of this family and cause separation and destruction. In a sense, he had us stuck in a "religious cult", which would only benefit him and blind fold Kay.

Arnold initially presented himself to be a "sheep" in white clothing, however he proved himself to be the devil in disguise. Arnold could read the bible front to back and tell you scripture after scripture. He was able to manipulate others into believing his bits and pieces he took from the bible for his own use. If you disagreed or tried to go against what he said, you were thrown out.

The first child to be thrown out of the house was Brian Jr., the only boy. Celeste's thoughts on this, is due to Arnold having seen Brian Jr. as a threat to "him" and his plan. Celeste and her other sisters were all very close to their brother Brian Jr., and the older girls Celeste, Mignon and Janelle expressed to their brother Brian Jr. that they did not feel comfortable around Arnold, and that they didn't like the way he looked at them, so when Brian Jr. tried to voice his concerns about what his sister had told him, it turned into a heated argument, which ultimately resulted in Brian Jr. being put out at the age of thirteen at five thirty in the morning, with nowhere to go. It was later discovered that Brian Jr. went to a homeless shelter for youth known as the Covenant House.

The abrupt exit of their brother caused Celeste and her other siblings to be heartbroken and mad, however felt they were stuck in a rut, for fears that they too would next be put out with nowhere to go or beaten. After a while, Celeste and her siblings could no longer take it anymore and started to rebel.

Celeste had mentioned to her mother the way Arnold use to look at her, and comment on her lower back side and breast in her clothing, however it feel on deaf ears. Kay's response to this was, "oh, you take

everything the wrong way, it's not like that", despite Celeste telling her that it made her feel uncomfortable, Kay could careless and only continue to think of herself. Celeste always felt that Kay never truly grew up and was still this young girl who never knew how to be a mother and accept responsibility.

Celeste believed that deep down, Kay always knew what Arnold was doing was wrong, yet she never did anything to protect her children. It was always more beneficial for her "needs" to be met and her being a priority, as opposed to her addressing her own children's needs and protecting them. She called Celeste a "problem child', who just didn't want her to be "happy".

Celeste tried to mention many times to her mother how when Arnold asked to take her out to run an errand with him, how he winded up at some hotel, trying to provide her alcohol and to smoke marijuana. Celeste also mentioned Arnold proceeded to massage her arms, breasts and then proceeded to try to insert his index finger in her vagina. It was at this point, that Celeste angrily asked him to stop. Celeste wanted him to stop all along, but desperately needed enough evidence to be able to tell her mother, in hopes that she would be able to finally listen.

But Kay didn't listen, instead she became infuriated with Celeste by the news she tried to share with her, and when this was brought her to attention, she argued that Celeste was just a "problem child' who did not want her to be happy, and that she wasn't t going allow her to ruin her happiness. Another mistake of Kay's. she would later find out, that Arnold's pedophilic behavior continued onto to her younger sibling sisters.

Chapter Five

I wish I could say things got better at this point; however, unfortunately, they only took a turn for the worse. After Celeste's concerns were fallen to the waist side by Kay, Arnold begin to pick up his tactics. He took the fourth child and third female daughter Janelle to a hotel, when she was just thirteen years old. Janelle kept this hidden for a few weeks, but her sister Celeste and Mignon noticed she was acting quite different and tried to limit her contact around Arnold.

Janelle also begin to not want to sleep in her room anymore by herself, and preferred sleeping all bunched together with her sisters Celeste and Mignon. Then one day, Janelle's sisters asked her about her recent strange behavior, and she shared with her sisters that Arnold had taken her to a hotel and was showing her pornography, she also shared that he was massaging her, telling her that he was massaging the "demons" out of her.

Celeste was infuriated at hearing this news, and she immediately confronted her mother with this. Kay's initial response she appeared to be infuriated, and even put Arnold out. It appeared as if she finally was going to do something and actually be a mother. However, Arnold kept calling her and begging for forgiveness. Him being out of the house was short-lived, a week at most.

Arnold and Kay sat Celeste and her siblings down with the excuse that Arnold was trying to "teach" Janelle about sex, because she was maturing. Janelle was only thirteen at the time. My thoughts were, shouldn't that be something her mother should be teaching her about?

However, Kay fell for that, and Arnold was yet allowed back in the home and in Celeste and her siblings' lives.

At this point, Celeste and her younger siblings no longer trusted him, and just trying to hold on as long as they could, until Celeste turned eighteen, with the hopes of Celeste getting a place and taking her siblings with her to live. However, after the incident that took place between Arnold and Janelle, she no longer felt comfortable to stay there, and ran away to stay with her friends.

Kay tried to call the police and make a report about Janelle leaving and trying to force her to come back; however that was only an effort to cover her, that she merely reported it. As a result of the report, Janelle was forced to come back, that time. Doesn't it appear to be funny how this same effort wasn't put out when Brian Jr. was put out?

But living in a home with Arnold was not easy. Celeste expressed that Arnold had total control of the house, due to him convincing Kay to leave her job and promising her that he would take care of the house, was yet another part of his "plan", to gain total control of the household, which he did.

Chapter Six

As time went on, things just got worst. Arnold managed to divide the family and separate Kay from all of her family and friends. One day, there was heated argument that broke out with Mignon and Arnold, and Kay intervened and because she didn't like the way Mignon was speaking to Arnold, she charged at her with a frozen soda can, and hit her upside her head, leaving a bruise on the side of her head. Mignon went on to school and as a result of this, Mignon was taken out of the house, along with Janelle. Arianna was not taken, because she was sent out of state, in an effort to avoid having to go into the system.

Mignon and Janelle were forced to stay in foster care for over a period of six months. The time they spent in foster care was one of the most difficult times in their lives and in Celeste's life. Celeste was able to escape foster care, as she was already staying with a close family friend, after being kicked out of the house after a physical altercation that took place with Arnold and Kay.

Luckily for Janelle and Mignon, they were able to stay with Celeste's aunt and Mignon's god-mother. After all of this happened, Kay complied with ACS mandates, ensured ACS that she would not allow Arnold to return when everything was revealed about his inappropriate behavior towards the girls, and so they were returned.

However, once again, that was short lived, and within less than a month, Arnold returned. Celeste also returned, only to be around to try and protect her younger siblings against Arnold. It was only a matter of time before Arnold resumed his inappropriate behavior again. Celeste

recounts a time when she woke up from her sleep to be startled by the presence of Arnold staring at her, and when asked why he was in her room, he said she needed to pray, because she had "demons" and was "playing with herself in her sleep".

Celeste knew this too be a lie, and it was later shared by her other siblings, that he had done the same thing to them as well, and had also told them the same story about them "playing with themselves". His perverseness was clearly getting worse and worse, with no intentions of stopping.

This was as result of Kay not putting a stop to his behavior from the beginning; his behavior began to increase over time, because he knew he could get away with it. Kay refused to believe any of her children, not because she didn't know it to be true, but simply because she did not want to interrupt "her" comfortable lifestyle.

Celeste mentions how she lost countless clothes, a television set and stereo she brought when she got her first job working at McDonald's due to being put out after arguments, from trying to tell Kay about Arnold's behavior. Arnold would always try to start an argument with one of the Kay's daughters, whenever they said they did not want to go "hang out "with him.

Arnold's definition of hanging out was trying to take people to hotels and offering alcohol and marijuana to underage children. Celeste mentions how Arnold once took her to hotel when she was just sixteen and showed her pornographic movies, then tried to massage her as well, stating he was massaging away the demons. Celeste knew this just didn't feel right, Celeste then mentions, that Arnold went into the bathroom and returned back completely naked and tried to perform oral sex on her, stating that he would rather her "learn" from him, that someone else.

Celeste mentions that when his advances were rejected, I guess he saw the fear and disgust in her eyes, in his sick twisted mind, he tells her that he needs to pray because he has demons, and apologizes to Celeste crying, yet then turns around and starts and argument and Celeste is put out yet again.

Chapter Seven

Celeste never mentioned anything that Arnold had did or said to her, due to shame and embarrassment. Celeste did however continue to go and back and forth from Kay's house in an effort to keep an eye on her youngest sisters who was still in the house, however it was always short lived.

The moment that Arnold's advances were refused, he always threatened to kick someone out, and always knew just how to start and argument.

The final draw for Celeste and that was final time that she left Kay and Arnold's house was when she Celeste had gotten pregnant with her daughter Danielle. By this time, Celeste was twenty. Arnold mentioned to Celeste the disappointment he felt of her getting pregnant, and that she could have borrowed "his dick", and then she wouldn't have gotten pregnant.

Some people may think that it's just words, however the words were disgusting and perverse, and brought all of the memories that this monster has brought amongst Celeste and her siblings. The horrific experiences that Celeste and her siblings had to encounter at such an early age. Having the experience of facing teenage homelessness, of not knowing where you're going to sleep at night and going from place to place. One night, Mignon experienced having to sleep in an unlocked vehicle, in the dead of winter, after having an argument with Kay about Arnold's behavior.

The other thing was losing important things, and missing out on special events. Like having to drop out of high school, and having to miss out on the experience of going to the junior prom and senior prom, simply because there was no stability in the lives of Celeste and her siblings. Celeste was unable to stay focused on keeping up with her studies and overall education, as a result of being unaware as to where she was going to lay her head every night. Fortunately, for Celeste, she was able to find refuge staying with her longtime friend and neighbor Tanya, who's mother allowed her to stay in her home with them.

None of these things were ever reported too authorities, until years later, due to Celeste and her siblings fears coming from Kay and Arnold, of the kids being put back into foster care. it was better to ride it out, until Celeste was able to get her own place, so she could take her siblings out to live with her, and that was exactly what Celeste had did.

Another turning point in the lives of Celeste and her sister Mignon, was years later after they found out that Arnold was also molesting their younger sister as well, Celeste and Mignon ran to their younger's sister defense, as a result, Kay had them arrested. This was both devastating and hurtful to both Celeste and Mignon. Not only the fact that their mother didn't believe them, or protect them from this predator, but when they tried to protect their sister from this, they were penalized for this. Celeste and Mignon agreed to the legal requirements as per their lawyer, in an effort to avoid having their permanent records affected, however they were still left feeling no sense of closure, and like their mother and the legal system had failed them.

Chapter Eight

Celeste went on to get her GED and was able to obtain during the same time she would have, as if she would have graduated from high school in 1996. From there, things begin to fall into place, Celeste later went on to get a job working in the post office and eventually got her own place. Working at the post office was enough to pay the bills, however it wasn't enough to fulfill her.

Celeste felt that the Creator had a "purpose" for her life. The old saying is that we never pass through anything in "vain" or just because, there is always a purpose. One of the many reasons I decided to a pursue a career in social work. There are so many people who suffer in silence with things similar having happened to them such as what happened to Celeste.

As mentioned earlier in this book, despite what has happened in your past, your past does not define who you are? There can and will be brighter days, What the devil meant to break you down and destroy you with, can ultimately be turned for good by helping someone else overcome.

It's only recently, Celeste began to speak out about what happened to her in her past, and those close family members and friends who knew about what Celeste and her siblings had to encounter throughout the years, ask the question quite often, why did you even keep going back and forgiving your mother for allowing this to happen to you? You only have one mother, children don't ask to come here, and I consider myself to be a family oriented person, one of the very reasons, Celeste

assumed the mother role for her siblings. We all have a desire to love and be loved, especially by our parents, regardless to how bad, good or indifferent they may be.

My only thought on this is, unfortunately we have no control or choice on who our parents are, but we do have a choice to provide forgiveness. Forgiveness doesn't mean you forget, it just means we take back control of our lives. The things that happen to Celeste as a child/adolescent was not due to "her control", because she had none, but she does have the choice to take it back.

When you forgive, you say I know you hurt me, but I'm going to forgive you for two reasons. The first reason is, because the Creator told me too, and the second reason is because, when you were younger, your control was taken from you, and now you are reclaiming it. The Creator has a way of balancing out the scales, and he will make it right.

Lastly, with forgiveness, also comes the restoration. In spite of your trials and tribulations, "joy cometh in the morning". I hope this book provides someone who may have experienced the same thing a sense of peace and comfort. You may ask yourself, hmm. Where is Celeste now? Well, Celeste has since went on to provide support and counseling and continues to advocate on behalf of victims of sexual abuse, molestation and assault for both and men, and has already begun the process of reaching out to politicians on all levels from federal, state and local governments, in an effort to change the statute of limitations for bringing perpetrators of these crimes to justice.

In NYS, after five years, you cannot bring a perpetrator of this crime to justice, yet the damaging effects that it has on the victims' lives, well outweighs the "five years". In fact, studies show that most victims who experience these crimes are fearful to come out and suffer in silence for many years, until they are adults and feel more comfortable to talk about it. Why should their crimes be limited to five years, when the damage they cause in the lives of their victims, supersedes that mark.

There are many reasons they suffer in silence, shame, embarrassment, fear, exploitation, etc.. Just because they remain silent, doesn't mean their pain is not there, nor or the memories or the PTSD. Celeste will continue on her journey to advocate for victims similar to herself.

Celeste has went on to obtain four degrees. Two masters degrees one in Criminal Justice, and one in Social Work. In addition, Celeste is currently enrolled in a doctorate program for Social Work. Celeste questioned the Creator many times, "why me"? She now knows as painful as and dark as those hours and days were in her life, it was necessary. It was all in preparation, ultimately for the purpose the Creator had in her life to help herself heal and others. Celeste continues to have an estranged relationship and no contact with Kay or Arnold, however Celeste continues to have a tight knit relationship with her siblings.

In closing, Celeste would like to reiterate to stay encouraged and empowered, you are no longer a victim, but you are a warrior. "YOU CAN, AND YOU WILL OVERCOME"!

I am a living witness to this, because I AM CELESTE!!

I wrote this book, due to my experience when I was in field work for social work school, and seeing how many people were suffering from various past trauma in their lives, and feeling a sense of hopelessness, because of their past. I'm hear to tell you your past, is just that, your "past". I wasn't born with a silver spoon, far from it, I had to struggle to get through. The average person would have probably just through their hands up, and gave up, but I didn't ,it only made me stronger. We all have a story in life, good, bad or indifferent, it isn't the end though. Don't seek closure from your abusers, or from whomever hurt you. Forgive for "YOURSELF", so you can "HEAL", and be able to move forward. REGAIN YOUR CONTROL", and let your voice be heard! This book isn't meant to bash anyone, because I have forgiven, and have chosen to eliminate those toxic individuals from my life. This book is a sense of freedom, empowerment and healing for myself, with the hopes of providing encouragement and healing to others. If I can do, I pray that you know and believe that the Creator can and will do it for you.

I pray for many blessings upon your lives and those of your loved ones. I pray that my book helps even one individual who is suffering with this, and then my job is done. Look out for book # 2, which will focus on getting rid of toxic people within your life, healing and self love.

CPSIA information can be obtained
at www.ICGtesting.com
Printed in the USA
BVHW081304050319
541823BV00003B/417/P

9 781796 016857